The Art of Self-Enquiry

Author

Penmetsa Venkata Satya Suryanarayana Raju

Dr.P.V.S.Suryanarayana Raju.

#5-8-16, Park street,Narsapur.

W.G.Dt, AP,INDIA.

Pin:534275.

Ph: 918814-273430.

Email: drrrajunsp@yahoo.co.in

Fax: 918814-277852.

Dedication.

This book is dedicated to

Bhagawan Sri Ramana Maharshi.

About the Author:

The author,Dr.P.V.S.Suryanarayana Raju is paediatrician from Andhra Pradesh,India,born on 12th December 1950.He is working on the subject of self-inquiry for the past 30 years under the living Presence and guidance of Ramana Maharshi which he discovered 30 years ago in Ramanasramam. He is a frequent visitor to Ramanasramam and out of greatfulness to Bhagawan he wrote many books analyzing his teachings and these books are some of them. His works include The Art of self-enquiry, Alpha and Omega of self-inquiry, The essence of self-inquiry part 1 & 2, Insights in self-inquiry Part 1 & 2,Theory of self-inquiry, The Practice of self-inquiry, The theory and Practice of self-inquiry, The comprehensive book on self-inquiry, Know Thyself, self-inquiry in yoga Vasista, Self-inquiry in Adi Sankara works, he wrote self-inquiry quotes in two volumes, commented on "who am i", Upadesa saram,Akshara Mana Malai of Ramana Maharshi and all are his products of his own experience. He wrote many books on Bhagawan in Telugu which include "Nenevadanu? which is a commentary of him on "who am i" in Telugu, Nija Vicharana and his most recent books in Telugu Vichara Chudamani, and Vichara Chandrodayam mainly deal with the practical aspect of self-inquiry and he explains in them why self-inquiry is a direct and easy way for realizing the Self. He also wrote self-inquiry in Bhagavad Gita,Bhagavad Gita commentary vol1,The essence of Bhagavad Gita. Inner conflict leads to outer disorder, Self-inquiry The Art of unveiling the Self.

Eka sloki of
Bhagawan sri Ramana Maharshi.

IN THE MIDDLE OF HEART CAVE THERE IS ONLY THE BRAHMAN.

THERE THE CONSCIOUSNESS IS PULSATING AS "I AM", "I AM" ONE CAN

ENTER THE HEART CAVE AND ABIDE THERE EITHER BY DELVING DEEP

INTO THE HEART BY SELF ENQUIRY OR BY STILLING THE VITAL AIRS
(PRANA).

Inquiry into the self is the most

Blissful activity of life because it

Is through which we realize the

Truth that one becomes capable of

Dropping all miseries. ~ Author.

Foreword

Majority of spiritual seekers feel that Self is something to be achieved. It is a misconception. Self is already the case but we are unable to feel its presence because it is clouded by thick clouds of conditioning born out of identity to the body, family, tradition, beliefs, dogmas, nationality, race, caste, creed, profession, gender, etc. Many feel that living a positive life means is to have more ambition, greed, arrogance, accumulating more knowing, always in a state of "becoming" which involves time. Actually these are all the signs of mental disorder and living with them leads to a life of conflict, contradiction, sorrow, despair and we are alienated from our own Self with such way of living. So it is a negative way of living and humanity is unfortunately conditioned in that way. Positive way of living involves a life of living in the present moment and act spontaneously. In this way we act from pure conscious without intermediary distortion of the ego. Life is action in relationship. So how we act is very important in determining the way of life. Because of Self ignorance we are acting from the ego, the "me" which is the summation of experiences born out of incomplete action. " Me" is limited and its action is limited leaving the residue of non-understanding in the form of experiences. They are stored in memory cells and thought arises from that center and we are acting from that center. So we facing ever changing reality from a fixed, dead past center. When act like that such action is naturally incomplete and brings us sorrow which is quite obvious if we observe our life. So there is a need to investigate into that urgently otherwise sorrow goes on accumulating. So in self-inquiry we go into the question why we are identifying with all these degenerating factors. Identity and ego are possible in a state of non-awareness of the activity of ego. In self-inquiry we do it with the light of awareness, and gradually the thick clouds of condition first become thin and finally disappear. When those clouds disappears we perceive Self-effulgent Self. S o in self inquiry the veil over Self is removed and our mind is posited in Self and we live a positive life with love, compassion.

The Author

Introduction

Self-inquiry is not difficult. Because of our conditioning it looks difficult to us. Daily we sleep and we are not aware of adjuncts like intellect, memory, ego, thinking process during sleep and it is in everybody's experience that we are very happy during deep sleep in which there is no limitation and so duality. But we are not enjoying this happiness while we are fully conscious. To know our nature of Self which is intrinsically happy even without any association with adjuncts is the Art of Self-inquiry. In deep sleep the adjuncts are in suspended animation and consciousness is pure in that state. So it is called Prajnana Ghana in Sanskrit. In deep sleep state there are no seer in the sense that there is nothing to be seen as objects with name and form. The seer and the seen are interrelated. If one of them is absent the other is also absent. They rise and disappear together. There is only one difference between deep sleep state(Sushpti) and Samadhi(Paralysis of activity of mind in waking mode of mind), in deep sleep we are unaware of Self but in Samadhi we are aware of Self in full consciousness. Attaining to Samadhi state of mind is the aim of all spiritual practices including Self-inquiry. While we are extremely happy in the non-dual state of sleep why that happiness is getting disturbed once we are awake from the sleep. So we have to investigate into those factors which are disturbing our intrinsically happy state of Self in waking mode of mind. Once we are awake in a split second our consciousness is getting identified with body-mind complex. Life with identity with body-mind complex is action in relationship. We cannot live in isolation, we have to live with fellow beings and nature. Even breathing is action. So if action in relationship ends life of body-mind complex ends. How is our relationship with the rest at present? If we are aware of the subject and the object simultaneously, in that mirror of relationship we will know the present status of our mind. This is possible when one is established as witnessor instead of identifying with the subject and thinking that awareness as "I am". Once we identify with the ego which is just a summation of al dead past experiences, life which is action is relationship is distorted because ego wants to save itself through ego activity and every action born out of ego circumscribes our consciousness which further strengthens the ego.Once consciousness is circumscribed there arises the duality of "me" and "not me" and there is perennial conflict between these thought fabricated entities and there is continuous wastage of energy and life. So to do an action which never brings any conflict in life we must have right thinking. Obviously right thinking is not possible from ego center because it itself is the result of conflict and its survival depends on conflict. If there is no conflict in life we don't need any ego. So for right thinking self knowledge is required. Many feel that self knowledge is impossible to gain but it is easier than acquiring skills in scientific knowledge because we require a great effort to accumulate scientific knowledge. Just to be aware of mind and its activities is self knowledge. It is an effortless process of understanding which comes about when one begins objectively and goes deeper and deeper into the whole problem of daily living which is relationship in action between you and me.

Human body-mind complex is a product of evolution. So it is time bound. When consciousness identifies with that complex duality and so conflict arises. All time bound entities are bound to be in conflict. Eternity, that which is beyond time integrates polarities of time bound entities and makes them complimentary to each other thus bringing integration as a unitary whole. Actually that is the work of biological mind to bring integration between polarities. Biological mind does not separates us from the rest. It is the ego which is dead memory and experience that separates one being from the other. When we give strength to the ego the natural flow of thought-feeling is blocked and we function from an abnormal center of ego and out thought process is perverted and directed against the fellow being and nature. Naturally this leads to pathological way of life which leads us to misery, conflict, contradiction. If we are aware of working of this pathological state of thinking, we have self knowledge, so right thinking, right action and so we lead a life of order in which love is intrinsic. Hate is intrinsic to a life of conflict, disorder. A life without love is not a life at all but humanity is leading a life of disorder and so hate. So everybody needs self-inquiry. Biological mind allow love to flow through it. Children before they are conditioned function from the biological mind and they are extremely happy and loving for no reason. Saints when they are fully free of conditioning function again from the biological mind and they are loving and blissful for no reason. That is why Jesus said unless you become children again you cannot enter the kingdom of God. This child-like innocent consciousness is possible when one is free of all tendencies and conditioning. If we are aware of this we can root out all tendencies from which all pathological thinking process is happening. If we don't give energy to tendencies and conditioning they die on their own because of lack of energy supply. To whatever we give energy they grow be it good or bad. If we don't give energy to anything we are left only with the Self and it is beyond all antinomies. A mind filled with such pure energy without any contents is the most powerful instrument of creation. Such a mind acts without any goal spontaneously. This is normal pristine state of any human being. Because rest are functioning with ego awareness which is actually a diseased state of mind, this natural state looks abnormal. To attain to this normalcy self-inquiry is a must. There is no other go. In other methods ego is nourished in the name of spirituality.

Self-consciousness- Object knowing consciousness.

The basic form of self consciousness "I am" underlies all these thee states of the mind. In the waking and dream states we superimpose adjuncts like body, intellect, thinking and object knowing upon our basic form of self consciousness "I am" and thus we experience self consciousness in a distorted way as "I-am-the-body", I am thinking, I am knowing. This adjunct bound, so limited distorted form of our self consciousness is a pseudo consciousness which is mind. The relationship between the self and the mind is like rope and snake, the snake is just we imagine to be. So all the three states of mind are mere imaginations. Self never becomes the mind.

Since the mind appears and disappears mind cannot be real. So anything known by it is not real. We witness the appearance and disappearance of the mind, we exist independent of it, hence mind as a seer(Jnata) cannot be the real "I".

When we experience content less state of deep sleep we do not experience body or mind, so the consciousness is adjunct less, so without any limitation, so it is self consciousness devoid of adjuncts except nescience(Avidya, Self-ignorance) which veils the light of self conscious being. In the waking state we mistake our mind and the gross body to be the "I". In the dream state we mistake our mind and subtle body to be the "I". In deep sleep state we mistake neither our mind nor body to be the "I" so the finite sense of "I" is devoid in deep sleep but we are under the influence of nescience(Avidya, lack of self-knowledge) in deep sleep. Yet all these three states are experienced by "I am ness" which underlies all these three states. Mind comes into existence by superimposing imaginary adjuncts on this basic consciousness of "I am". That which really knows that I was asleep is not our mind but our real self consciousness. Mind usurps the experience and say "I know that i was asleep".

Deep sleep is something where we do not exist as mind. Deep sleep is thought action free state. Just because we do not do anything in deep sleep we should not conclude that we do not exist or do not know anything. In deep sleep we have the knowledge of nothingness i.e absence of objective knowledge due to the absence of mind. To know nothingness there must be consciousness, so sleep is a part our conscious experience like waking and dream states and the undercurrent of self consciousness "I am" is there in all these three states. If we are devoid of all consciousness it is not possible to know the deep sleep state at all. What enables us to cognize the sleep is the perpetual continuity of our fundamental self consciousness "I AM" which endures uninterrupted through all these states. Self-enquiry is a nonobjective state in which that which attends is itself that which attends to. Our aim is to hold this type of uncontaminated pure self conscious blissfully aware being.

Self-inquiry is real religiosity.

A religious person is one who sets out search for his "I" and more he goes on searching, the more he finds out that his "I" is not there at all. The day the shadow of "I" disappears, the day neither "I" or "you" remains, you will be pulled into the Self with it's magnetic effect. Then you feel at home for the first time. At present you are mistaking workshop of mind for your home and you are identifying with the utilitarian body- mind complex and suffering from uninterrupted mental conflict because of this wrong identity. So we have to find our real home through Self-Enquiry with awareness as the basis for investigation. If we live in the mind thinking that it is our home, there is continuous chattering interrupting our innate peace. There is anxiety, worry, tension, anguish, misery, suffering, desires etc and all these create many, many layers of curtain around the consciousness making it to appear cloudy, and you cannot feel at home because of them. These disturb the joy, peace, blissfulness which is our innate nature.

At present we are experiencing the things in unawareness and we go on repeating the same mistake again and again. That is why history repeats itself. If we are aware during an experience, we will not repeat the same mistake again. If we comprehensively encounter one experience in awareness, we develop the capacity to face any situation and there is the flowering of the art of Self-Enquiry. This is the real religiosity. Wrong belief that we are not the Self which leads us to identity with the body-mind complex will continuously obstruct, negate and closes the doors to all possibilities of flowing of light and energy of Self. The creative energy of Self is plugged, blocked and diverted to some activity that society thinks is going to pay.

In Self-inquiry one should not judge his mind, instead one should love it, by just witnessing it, then only the mind reveals it's content in the awareness and withers. During this de-structuring of mind in awareness there is pain of disillusionment because so far we thought ego is is our real home and leaving it now causes pain. One has to pass through this pain of disillusionment before transcending pleasure-pain ego life.

In the awareness of Self-Enquiry, one will purify himself of all wrong conditionings and auto suggestions. Self-Enquiry is an act of witnessing consciousness. The life you have so far lived is a long pretension of things that are not. For example one talks about compassion, universal brotherhood,

service to humanity etc keeping intact the ego with it's intrinsic separative feeling. These pretensions veil on your essential Self. You go on acquiring more veils in the form of knowledge, learning, scholarship etc. But Self-Enquiry is not a question of learning, it is an art perceiving the things "as they are", it is an act of knowing which is verbal in nature. It is just witnessing the inner chattering of mind with love. Everything, that which is not, disappears if you are aware, so also the inner chattering. When inner chattering stops even for few moments, you feel at home.

Whenever inner chattering starts again simply "be aware", the inner chattering stops and you will suddenly feel at home. This is Self-Enquiry.

Once the mind understands that you have found something greater, something better, something higher, slowly it recedes. It's function is fulfilled.

Now the mind is inward turned. It's activity is is a hurdle now.

When your mind is silent without any activity of thought, you will at home anywhere and you will be in tune with the whole. Gradually the awareness spreads slowly during sleep also and your whole energy is turned into silent pool without any ripples. Then there is no need to crave for anything including the hope for God, liberation. Then you will just "be" which is synonymous of "being the Self". This is real Self-Enquiry and real religiosity.

The need for self-inquiry in daily life.

Everybody needs sleep for his survival. If a man does not have sleep adequately he will go insane and his life will be in disorder. Similarly everybody needs meditation in waking state, otherwise his mind and life will be in disorder. This disorder is quite obvious both inside the mind and so outside in the present world where majority humanity have no idea or time to do meditation.

Meditation is to go beyond thought and establish ourselves in the being. But we cannot go beyond thought the mechanics of the working of the "me" which is an isolating and destructive factor. At present thought is dominating and directing our way of life.

Thought is a reaction of past memories and experiences and if it is face the challenge in the present which is always new, it encounters it partially which results in conflict.

So thought as our master of life brings disaster and ego is nothing but thought.

So thought subsides when activity of "me" subsides which is the result of understanding born out of awareness, watchfulness in a state of observation in which there is not a trace of condemnation or justification of what is being observed.

In that passive alertness we listen to the noise of the "me" with relaxed attention beyond the noise of words without intervening screen of thoughts, conclusions, prejudices.

The search for truth is individual and is not possible in religious congregations.

All this is possible in self-inquiry in which we go beyond thought and establish in the being and we respond to the challenge in a holistic way and we attend to the present

instead of getting lost in imagination of day dreaming and we relax totally in being in full awareness.

The Art of approaching the ego.

The approach to learn are diametrically opposite in physical and psychological fields. When we want to learn something in the physical world the process of recognition, experience, gaining knowledge and accumulating that knowledge experience in the memory cells of brain and responding from that accumulated knowledge and experience is key for growth in science, technology, learning a skill, learning a language etc. Here we have to use thought to get understanding and skill.

self-inquiry implies psychological learning. Many apply the above said method for learning about the mind which is self-inquiry or when we relate to other person we want to learn the relationship through thought which demand learning through experience of life which inevitably leads to residue of non-understanding leading to psychological conflict. This is because when we try to learn through thought which is a response of memory and memory being limited its response of thought is also limited which always leads to residue of non-understanding and conflict.

There is really no line of demarcation between physical learning and psychological learning and often there is overlap of the two.

In self-inquiry what we are concerned is about psychological learning that we have acquired through centuries or inherited as tradition, as knowledge, as experience. This we call learning, is it learning at all? that is the question. Mind has learned and with what it has learned it meets the challenge of life. It is always translating the life which is a flow of new challenges according to what it has learned. That is what we are doing, is it learning? Ego process is a dynamic entity, it acquires new experiences and sheds some experiences all the time. To learn about a living, dynamic entity like that we require an un-conditioned consciousness which is in a state of not knowing, without any preconceived ideas, beliefs, dogmas, and without any evaluation or judging what it sees.

Learning implies something new, something i don't know and am learning. If i am merely adding to what I already know it is no longer learning. If you are to discover for yourself what is the new, truth being always fresh and new, it is no good carrying the burden of the old, especially the knowledge, the knowledge of scripture or another person however great. A man protecting himself constantly through knowledge is obviously not a truth seeker.

When you want to find something new the mind must be quiet. If the mind is crowded filled with facts, knowledge, they act as as impediment to know the new.

The difficulty for most of us is that thought has become so important, so predominantly significant that it interferes constantly with anything that may be new, with anything that may exist simultaneously with the known. The knowledge and accumulative learning which involve time are impediments for those who would seek and try to understand that which is timeless. So one has to learn the skill of using thought in physical dimension and set aside all knowledge and experience when one wants learn about the ego which is always possible when we relate to the other. So when we relate to the other we must be watchful of our own ego without allowing the interference of thought.

So approaching the physical dimension is through thought and approach in the psychological dimension is watchfulness, witnessing without interference of thought. So we must note that approach is diametrically opposite in learning in physical dimension which is time bound and learning in psychological dimension which is not time bound.

self-inquiry is not an effort against the mind but rather a loving way of witnessing the mind which is the result of evolution and contains the whole experience of existence. Your mind is not personal, it represents the whole evolutionary process. So self-inquiry is an impersonal way of exploring the mind without any reference centre. Inquiring mind penetrates into itself, aware of one's own psychological being with its urges, compulsions, frustrations, desire to fulfil, miseries, strains, anxieties, struggles, sorrows and other innumerable problems. In self-inquiry there must be constant and earnest awareness.

Bhagawan never advised accumulation of information in the name of spirituality. His method is self-inquiry which is a process of de-learning and throwing contents of the mind through understanding. Every other spiritual methods require the "me" to do it. Majority of spiritual techniques involve doing in some form or the other. But Realization of Self is not an outcome of any "doing". In self-inquiry we don't depend on the "me" and on the contrary we question the very integrity of the "me". So a serious seeker of self-inquiry does not indulge in accumulation of information in the name of spirituality. It is quite surprising that genius of India opted to inquire into the self rather than running for material gains.

The entity that is investigated in Self-inquiry.

We have to investigate whether there is such an entity as the "thinker", the "me" as noun apart from thought. If we remove all thoughts from the thinker does an entity, as "thinker" remain? So thought is the thinker. One part of the mind assumes the role of thinker and it feels it is separate from other thoughts. Is the thinker separate from thought? We have to investigate. As the "I-am-the-body" idea is the root of all thoughts we have to investigate whether identity with the body through "I-am-the-body" idea is existential or not. This is important to investigate. Once we start investigating we bring awareness into the investigation and in the presence of awareness thought flow is reduced and finally comes to a standstill. Then we develop the capacity to hold on to "I-am-the-body" idea. Pure "I-am-the-body" idea is filled with pure awareness. It is not an obstruction to the revelation of self-knowledge. We can hold on to pure "I-am-the-body" idea in the interval between the transition of mind from one mode to another or in the interval between two thoughts. Then investigation becomes a piece of cake because there is no clouding of consciousness by thoughts in that interval. Till then we fall back into unawareness due to strong mental habits which are called tendencies even while doing self-inquiry. So uninterrupted Self-awareness (sada apramada) is needed for self inquiry.

self-inquiry demands psychological energy. But the energy is destroyed, is wasted when one is in conflict. So when there is the understanding of the whole process of conflict, there is the ending of conflict, there is abundance of energy. Then you can proceed, tearing down the house that you have built throughout the centuries and that has no meaning at all. You know, to destroy is to create. We must destroy the psychological, the unconscious and the conscious defences, securities that one has built up rationally, individually, deeply, and superficially. We must tear through all that to be utterly defenceless, because you must be defenceless to love and have affection. Then you see and understand ambition, authority; and you begin to see when authority is necessary and at what level -the authority of the policeman and no more. Then there is no authority of learning, no authority of knowledge, no authority of capacity, no authority that function assumes and which becomes status. To understand all authority -of the gurus, of the Masters, and others- requires a very sharp mind, a clear brain, not a muddy brain, not a dull brain.

The word "diving" is appropriate when there are outgoing tendencies, and when, therefore, the mind has to be directed and turned within, there is a dip below the surface externalities. But when quietness prevails without obstructing the Consciousness, where is the need to dive?

Humanity is in dark state of Self-ignorance. Ego is a product of this Self-ignorant dark state and the god, religion, poetry, art, painting it creates are all outcome of this darkness. The culture of human society, its education, family system, beliefs, dogmas all add to this metaphysical sleep and keeps the human in darkness causing lot of misery to him. Because ego state is a dark state we have to bring in light of "awareness" to know how the the ego is working and causing suffering to humanity. For this self-inquiry is the direct method and this book deals with that study of self. self-inquiry demands psychological energy. But the energy is destroyed, is wasted when one is in conflict. So when there is the understanding of the whole process of conflict, there is the ending of conflict, there is abundance of energy. Then you can proceed, tearing down the house that you have built throughout the centuries and that has no meaning at all. You know, to destroy is to create. We must destroy the psychological, the unconscious and the conscious defences, securities that one has built up rationally, individually, deeply, and superficially. We must tear through all that to be utterly defenceless, because you must be defenceless to love and have affection. Then you see and understand ambition, authority; and you begin to see when authority is necessary and at what level -the authority of the policeman and no more. Then there is no authority of learning, no authority of knowledge, no authority of capacity, no authority that function assumes and which becomes status. To understand all authority -of the gurus, of the Masters, and others- requires a very sharp mind, a clear brain, not a muddy brain, not a dull brain. Is there an action not of desire? If we ask such a question, and we rarely do, one can probe, without any motive, to find an action which is of intelligence. The action of desire is not intelligent; it leads to all kinds of problems and issues. Is there an action of intelligence? One must always be somewhat sceptical in these matters; doubt is an extraordinary factor of purification of the brain, of the heart. Doubt, carefully measured out, brings great clarity, freedom. In the Eastern religions, to doubt, to question, is one of the necessities for finding truth, but in the religious culture of Western civilization, doubt is an abomination of the devil. But in freedom, in an action that is not of desire, there must be the sparkle of doubt. When one actually sees, not theoretically nor verbally, that the action of desire is corrupt, distorted, the very perception is the beginning of that intelligence from which action is totally different. That is, to see the false as the false, the truth in the false, and truth as truth. Such perception is that quality of intelligence which is neither yours nor mine, which then acts. That action has no distortion, no remorse. It doesn't leave a mark, a footprint on the sands of time. That intelligence cannot be unless there is great compassion, love, if you will. There cannot be compassion if the activities of thought are anchored in any one particular ideology or faith, or attached to a symbol or to a person. There must be freedom to be compassionate. And where there is that flame, that very flame is the movement of intelligence.

We are so engrossed with the objects or appearances revealed by the light, that we pay no attention to the light. In the waking or dream state in which things appear, and in the sleep state in which we see nothing, there is always the light of Consciousness or Self, like the hall lamp which is always burning. The thing to do is to concentrate on the seer and not on the seen, not on the objects, but on the Light which reveals them.

 "What is the meaning of this talk of truth and falsehood in the world which is itself false?"

self-inquiry are very useful for any serious truth seeker irrespective of his background, conditioning, belief, faith, religion to which he belongs. self-inquiry is a scientific inquiry into the working of self, usually called the ego the ego, its thoughts, feelings etc. self-inquiry is beyond all religions in which there is no seeking, no becoming, no end to be gained. In the silent observation of self-inquiry in which there no choice or condemnation thought and feeling unfold themselves. In this process we actualize the potential of the Self (Atman).In self-inquiry we understand ourselves, our impulses, reactions, the whole process of thinking, conscious as well as unconscious/Depending on somebody to tell what is in our mind prevents understanding of oneself. Usually we take some shelter under an authority, be it a guru, scripture, method, which gives temporary sense of security, a sense of well being but that is not understanding of total process of oneself. Unless we uncover all the layers of mind including its unconscious part we will not have self-knowledge and creativity.

self-inquiry is a vital subject in life. Many human problems can be traced back to wrong identity with beliefs, dogmas, nationality, language, religion, colour of skin, race, profession, gender etc. If we are free of these identities we will relate to the other with a fresh mind without any prejudice, conclusion .Life is relationship with the other and we learn the "Art of living" through self-inquiry.

We are all conscious beings identified with the body-mind complex which is a product of time, of craving, of becoming. When we are dissociated with the body mind complex in deep sleep we are enjoying the tranquillity, peace, bliss, joy of our being. So the peace of our being is not the result of any effort or discipline. On the contrary when the thought subsides whatever is the cause there is the experiencing of joy. To enjoy that bliss in the waking mode of mind is the aim of all spiritual disciplines. But unfortunately all spiritual disciplines are based on thought and bliss is never the result of effort of thought. Once when the author went to darshan of a saint his completely subsided in the "presence" of saint. Then he understood for the first time that we can "be" in the absence of thoughts. He is more alive and joyful in that thought-free state of "being". He is very joyful for a couple of weeks due to that effect but later thought dominated as usual though his understanding of " being" is radically changed. By birth all beings including the human beings are dependent on the outer for food, shelter, clothing on the outer. We have to acquire them by effort. So physical survival depends on this acquisitive effort of thought. Because of lack of Self knowledge every being without exception searches for happiness in the outer using thought. Then pleasure is happiness. Pleasure means sensation, trying to achieve something through the body which is not possible to achieve through the body, forcing the body to achieve something it is not capable of. People are trying, in every possible way, to achieve happiness through the body. The body can give you only momentary pleasures, and each pleasure is balanced by pain in the same amount, in the same degree. Each pleasure is followed by its opposite because body exists in the world of duality, just as the day is followed by night and death is followed by life and life is followed by death. It is a vicious circle. Your pleasure will be followed by pain; your pain will be followed by pleasure. Buddha calls this the wheel of birth and death. We go on moving in this wheel, clinging to the wheel... and the wheel moves on. Sometimes pleasure comes up and sometimes pain comes up, but we are crushed between these two rocks. This moment is all. Now is the only time and here is the only space. And then suddenly the whole sky drops into you. This is bliss. This is real happiness. The essence of religiosity is witnessing in passive state of being, it is not thinking, it is not an effort. We innocently observe the activity of little self in self-inquiry.

Open your inner living book of ego which is not yet opened in you and its pages are uncut. Please don't die as an unopened book for it is sad that millions die as unopened books. Watch your own actions, relationships and moods more closely. Watch how you are when you are alone, how you are when you are with people, how you behave, how you react, whether your reactions are past oriented, follow a fixed pattern of thought or you are spontaneous. This book helps you to read your own book and helps you to go deeper into your own being, which is godliness, the Ultimate reality.

Witnessing in Self-inquiry.

self-inquiry is not an effort against the mind but rather a loving way of witnessing the mind which is the result of evolution and contains the whole experience of existence. Your mind is not personal, it represents the whole evolutionary process. So self-inquiry is an impersonal way of exploring the mind without any reference centre. Inquiring mind penetrates into itself, aware of one's own psychological being with its urges, compulsions, frustrations, desire to fulfil, miseries, strains, anxieties, struggles, sorrows and other innumerable problems. In self-inquiry there must be constant and earnest awareness.

Bhagawan never advised accumulation of information in the name of spirituality. His method is self-inquiry which is a process of de-learning and throwing contents of the mind through understanding. Every other spiritual methods require the "me" to do it. Majority of spiritual techniques involve doing in some form or the other. But Realization of Self is not an outcome of any "doing". In self-inquiry we don't depend on the "me" and on the contrary we question the very integrity of the "me". So a serious seeker of self-inquiry does not indulge in accumulation of information in the name of spirituality. It is quite surprising that genius of India opted to inquire into the self rather than running for material gains.

Accumulative learning- Learning by perception.

Basically there are two kinds of learning

1)   Accumulation of knowledge, of experience, of technology, of a skill, of a language. It is time bound.

2)   Psychological learning—learning through experience either through the immediate experiences of life which leave a certain residue of non-understanding, of tradition, of race, of the society. There is no line of demarcation between the two types of learning, they overlap. What we are concerned in self-inquiry is psychological learning that we have acquired through centuries or inherited as tradition, as knowledge, as experience. This we call learning, is it learning at all? Mind has learned and with what it has learned it meets the challenge of life in the active present. It is always translating the life or the new challenge according to what it has learned. This is what we are doing in the name of learning. Is that learning? Does not learning imply something new, something I don't know and am I learning if I am merely adding to what I already know, then it is no longer learning. If you are to discover for yourself what is the new, it is no good carrying the

burden of the old, especially the knowledge of scriptures or a great master.A man protecting himself constantly through such knowledge is obviously not a truth seeker. When you want to find something new, the mind must be quiet. If the mind is crowded, filled with the facts and borrowed knowledge they act as the impediment to the new. The difficulty for most of us is that the mind i. e thought has become so important, so predominantly significant that it interferes constantly with anything that may be new, with anything that may exist simultaneously with the known. Thus borrowed knowledge and learning are impediments for those who would seek, for those who would try to understand that which is beyond thought and so timeless and eternal.

Chapter8- Recognize that present way of living is bringing us sorrow.

 We do not know who we are, so we do not know what we are doing. Wherever you are you are missing your goal, your target. You don't know who you are, you don't know why you are, you don't know where you are headed -- and for what. Then only the door opens for growth, then suddenly you start looking in another dimension. Then you don't look out, you start looking in because whatsoever you do outside will lead you more and more away. The more you chase shadows outside, the more you will be losing yourself in the world. One starts closing one's eyes, one starts feeling and touching one's being. The first thing to know is 'who am I?' -- everything else is secondary. And if this basic thing is solved, if this basic problem is solved, if this basic mystery is penetrated, then all else is solved automatically. And if you don't solve this, and you don't answer the basic quest of man -- 'Who am I?' -- 'then whatsoever you do is irrelevant.   What are you doing? You are not trying to realize yourself, you are trying to compete with others. Nobody is trying to be oneself, everybody is trying to defeat the other. The whole world lives like a competitive madhouse. Man as he is, is simply living in a dream -- the dream of the ego, ambition, power, prestige. The man of wisdom is one who has come to understand that all this is going away from his centre. And it is easier to drop the past than to renovate it. It is easier to be completely cut off from the past rather than to modify it. You can paint a foolish thing, you can modify it, but you cannot make it wise -- it will remain foolish. It is better to drop it. So if this recognition has come to you that we are astray, feel blessed, and don't forget it. Remember it continuously. Unless you have come back to the path, go on remembering it. Just recognizing it once won't do, you will have to live it, remember it for a long time continuously, again and again, so the hammering continues -- whatsoever you have done in the past, it is finished. At least if you remember that it was all wrong... and I say all wrong. Don't try to decide that a few things were good. I insist: either all things are wrong or all things are right. There is no other way. It is not possible that a foolish man can do a few things that are right. And the vice versa is also not possible that a wise man can do a few things that are wrong. A wise man does all right and a fool goes on doing all wrong. But the fool would like to choose at least a few things right, the fool would say,' Yes, I have done many things wrong, but not all.' Then those things that he saves and says were right will become the centre for his ego again. So be totally frustrated with your past. The whole past was wrong, you simply drop it.

Body-mind complex.

. If an ordinary man says "I" he is referring with reference point of body-mind complex. Even when he says "you" he is using the same reference point. But a man endowed with Self knowledge knows that he is Pure conscious being, living in the body for the time being. When he says "I' his reference point is Pure consciousness. Because they have no separate feeling with the existence, they do not consider as non-self. Thiers's is a holistic life ,uniomystica. For those who are identified with their body-mind complex and feel that it is their essential being, for explanation purpose Pure consciousness is referred to as Self and the adjuncts and the world as "not-I" or "non-Self". This type of division helps the truth seeker to intellectually comprehend the fact that he is not just the body-mind only and this is called Parokshanubhuti (Indirect knowing of Self through intellectual understanding) .So this type of people never had direct experience of Self so far. That which can be seen is termed as non-Self and that which cannot be seen and not possible to show in the relative reality is termed Self. The annihilation of identity with the non-self happens in a split second in Toto but not as step by step. Though one tastes the Self, the grip of tendencies which is there from aeons and aeons of time not easily destroyed. So the mind which tastes the bliss of Self once uses all its energy to bail out from the grip of tendencies and it stops giving energy to those tendencies. Exactly these are the right people to do self-inquiry. The aim of self-inquiry is to know what we are not. There is no need to find what we are, it always exists as naturally as it should be. When we negate the not-I, we are left with "what we really are." It is just like sculpting a stone in which the unnecessary parts are removed and finally the idol is left with. So self-inquiry is a process of negation, a process of de-conditioning and de-structuring of the ego rather than a process of positive assertion that I am the Self.

Body:

It can be seen, it has six modifications (Shadbhava vikara) 1)Birth, 2) Exists for certain period only 3) Grows 4) changes 5) reducing 6) Finally death. When connected to mind the body functions through senses. When in deep sleep when it is disconnected with senses and mind in deep sleep it lies like dead body but for presence of vital functions like respiration and heart beat. So gross body has its existence only in the waking mode of the mind. So it is not our essential nature.

Senses:

They function in waking and dream mode of the mind. They are in suspended animation in deep sleep. So they are not our essential nature.

The mind:

We usually say today my mind is not peaceful, in conflict etc. So the mind is an object to witness. Mind is vulnerable to modifications and we are the witness to all these modifications of the mind. So our essential nature is not the mind.

The intellect:

It is common to say today my intellect is dull or mercurial. So we are the witness to the intellect and so it is not our essential nature.

Self-Ignorance

All the above said are result of Self-ignorance which knows not its nature. "I-am-the-body" idea arises from

Self-ignorance. It is just a conduit through which the power and bliss of Self passes into channels of the adjuncts. Because of association of the Self and its power, the products of Self-ignorance appear to be living and real but the adjuncts are different from the Self though the self and adjuncts appear to be inseparable. Adjuncts are not self revealing, just because of association with the reflected consciousness they appear to be independent living sentient entities but they are insentient by their very nature. Only Self is sentient. All others are insentient including Maya. With self-inquiry when we negate the not-I, self revealing real "I" found with its self effulgence. Then we directly perceive the Self without any aid of adjuncts and mind turns inward. This direct perception of Self is called Aparokshanubhuti in Vedantic jargon. Once the mind tastes the bliss of Self it loses interest in the objects of the phenomenal reality. Then we know directly know that Self appears as world when seen through the delusive mind. In the presence of power of magnet needles move but magnet has no modification whatsoever. We must divert our attention from adjuncts which are like those moving needles to the unmoving, one without any modification i.e witnessing consciousness. For this self-inquiry is the best way.

That which gives light and energy to all the adjuncts thus it is the cause of their animation is self-effulgent Pure consciousness.

The light in the Drama theatre helps us to see and identify actors and the witnessors of the drama. Even when the drama is over when the actors and the witnessors are gone the light continues to glow and shows us nobody is there. Similarly in the drama house like gross body the witnessor is Jnata (Seer, observer) ,the reflected consciousness is the king, Mind is the executive chief (Pradhan) ,the five vital airs are king's followers, senses are dancers (taladharas) five vital elements are seers of drama, intellect is heroin. All of them are present in waking and dream mode of mind .Jnata (The seer) shows all of them to us. When all of them are absent in deep sleep it shows us nothing-ness (Shunyata) to us. Being of the nature of witness it is beyond all modifications The seer belongs to Pure nature. (Sattwa, Para Prakruti) and the seen belongs to nature that is mixed with adjuncts.(Malina sattwa,Apara Prakruti). The awareness beyond the seen and the seen, observer and the observed is your essential nature.

The mind contains five vital physical principles in subtle form. In combination with the reflected consciousness (The seer,Jnata) it has the capacity to perceive the things in the objective reality. It has no capacity to comprehend the Pure consciousness.

Pure consciousness is not physical and so the mind cannot perceive and categorize it. Spiritual can feel the Pure consciousness. Because it is self effulgent and self revealing no adjunct is needed to know it. Consciousness at rest is called Pure consciousness, if the same consciousness starts moving with dynamism it is called Sakti. So what exists is only consciousness with different frequencies.

When consciousness enters the three principles of composure (Sattwa), active (Rajas) ,Inert (Tamas) creation happens. The three principles constitute Maya which is the power of Self. So what exists is only Self.

When we are in the grip of Maya we forget that we are the Self. When the mind is attracted by the things in objective reality it moves. Movement is its nature. If it becomes still it becomes one with the reality.

Self Knowledge

When the world which is what-is-seen has been removed, there will be realization of the Self which is the seer.

When a drop of ocean of Pure consciousness forgets its nature due to the action of Maya it is called Self-ignorance.(Avidya). The gross manifestation of Self-ignorance is the waking mode of mind. When the reflected consciousness is veiled due to veiling effect of Maya we forget that we are the Self. Due to the defect of multiplicity (Vikshepa Dosha) the unitary veiled thing appears as multiple. Then the active principle (Rajas) in association with the reflected consciousness takes the form of "I" thought, the ego and the inert principle in association with reflected consciousness appears as the world. With the separate feeling like this the seer sees the seen in a relative manner.

The basic form of pure consciousness is self effulgent and self revealing. But limited consciousness is Self-ignorant and so there is volition and doubt from which thought clouds arise and those thick layers of clouds hinder us from gaining Self knowledge. In waking mode of mind there is misery of bondage and desire for release from that bondage. When we inquire into the entity that feels it is in bondage, that entity disappears. Because Self is self effulgent, there is nothing like seer, seen, seeing as in case of relative world. If mind stops moving the Self reveals. Initially the Self reveals in the waking mode, later it reveals in an uninterrupted way in all the modes of mind. With the action of grace if we do self-inquiry our mind will be in the grip of Self. Self-inquiry becomes easy in the presence of the master.

In twilight rope appears as snake. In bright light rope appears as rope and delusory knowledge of snake is annihilated. As long as rope appears as snake, rope is not seen. Due to delusion rope appears as snake. Similarly when Brahman appears as the world, there is no revelation of Brahman. When self effulgent Brahman appears world is not perceived in the present form.

In waking mode and dream mode of mind we perceive the world with name and forms. In deep sleep mode of mind neither the world with name and form nor Brahman is perceived. In Samadhi mode of mind the mind enjoys the bliss of the ultimate reality but the world is not perceived.

When light passes through a prism we perceive seven colours but the original light has nothing to do with those seven colors. Similarly when the Pure consciousness pass through the filter of mind the composure (sattwa) element appears as god, the active principle (Rajas) appears as the Individual (Jiva) consciousness and the inert principle (Tamas) appears as the world. It is all mental creation. So mind is a compound and qualified consciousness. Pure consciousness has nothing to do with these mental creations. Though the world is a consciousness in movement when seen with the mind, it appears according to the state of the mind. For ordinary people with limited consciousness it appears as the world of name and form, for Self realized souls it appears as Brahman. The world of name and form and its inertness is a creation of the mind. Unless the mind creation subsides world will not appear as Brahman. When the consciousness passes through the mind we don't see the things "as they really are". Seeing the reality as multiplicity is evolution. In Samadhi mode mental creation stops and so world of names and forms is not seen, only Pure Maya reflecting the reality is there. Creative capacity of Maya is real but its creation is delusory because creation is not to be seen with the advent of Samadhi.

The existence of the world and mind are conceptual superimposed knowledge on the substrate of Brahman. If the knowledge of rope is there the delusory knowledge of snake will not be there. The mind and the world belong to a fabricated superimposed knowledge category and so they disappear with the knowledge of Brahman. That which disappears at any time, with any thing is not true.

Mind is a progeny of self-ignorance and when we see Brahman with the mind it appears as the world in present state. But when seen with the eyes of Self knowledge world appears as Brahman. Superimposed knowledge is false but the substrate real. Delusion never happens in the absence of substrate.

Mind is present in waking and dream modes of mind only. It is absent in Samadhi and deep sleep states, But we are taking the knowledge of waking mode as real and as reference point. With such attitude we will never find Brahman.

No Mind state(Biological Mind)

No mind Amanaska state is our natural state. The states with mind are unnatural. So melting the mind in spiritual heart is the aim of self-inquiry. Once one discovers that he is a conscious being he finds consciousness even in insentient things. So only after the superimposed knowledge is annihilated the knowledge of the substrate Brahman is revealed to us.

When the mind subsides, the world subsides. They are interdependent. Such is their relation.

Ego is thought. If there is no thought, there is no activity of ego. Ego appears to be there when thought activity is there. When thought completely subsides a state called Mruta Manas (No Mind state, Amanaska sthithi) happens.

The mind perceives and experiences the objects in the phenomenal reality. When the experiencing of the object is over, the memory of it is stored as experience in the brain cells. This is the normal function of the biological mind. In this there is no identity of mind with anything and flow of thought-feelings is not obstructed at any time This is called Aham Vrutti in which the mind is just aware that it is living in a body without any identity with it. When mind gets identified with the body, there is obstruction to the natural flow of thought-feeling and ego centre is formed around the "I-am-the-body" idea. So all thoughts are dependent on this " I-am-the-body" idea but the mother thought "I-an-the-body" idea is not dependent on other thoughts. Bhagawan tells us to hold this mother thought in self-inquiry. When the mother is held in awareness it is disconnected with the other thoughts and it becomes "Pure-I –am-the-body" idea which is devoid of identity with anything like body, belief, dogma etc. When we can hold this "Pure-I-am-the body" idea because it is not devoid of any identity it flows towards its source of Self. So actually Pure "I-am-the body" idea is a major aid to discover the Self during self-inquiry.

Action with Doer-Ship.

But when there identity with anything in any form doer is born. That doer is the ego. Doer is more concerned with enjoying the fruit of action than doing the action for action sake. In this way doer-ship and enjoyer-ship are born. At present action is proceeding from the Self-ignorant state of ego in which there is prejudice, tendencies, craving which result in sorrow. So ego is both discernment and action. There is constant interaction between those cravings, prejudices, tendencies and limitations which action is creating, in such context the ego process is born. Personality is a series of self imposed limitations, a series of accumulative actions, of hindrances which gives rise to consciousness the identity called "Ego". It is a series of memories, tendencies, which are born of cravings and our present action is a friction between craving and its object.

Action is the result of prejudice, fear, belief and such action produces further limitation. If we are raised in particular belief or tendency it must create a resistance against the movement of life. These resistances are self protective egoistic walls of security and gives rise the birth of ego process which is maintaining itself through its own activities. So in self-inquiry you must be aware of this process of building up of "false I". This process has no beginning, yet by constant awareness and by right effort it can be brought to an end. The art of self-inquiry demands a way of life to bring this ego process to an end. Once mind tastes the bliss of Self it immediately loses interest in things in the objective reality which may give pleasure which is transient by its nature and so painful. The bliss of Self has no opposite state to it. It is beyond all antinomies like pain/pleasure. With the subsidence of thought there is subsidence of mind with its senses and subsidence of the world that is perceived in the present form.

The gross (karmendriyas) and subtle senses (Jnanendriyas) are adjuncts that help us to function in the objective reality.

Mind is the inner adjunct and chief senses which presides over the function of body-mind complex.

Its decisive function is called intellect. (Buddhi)

The entity which creates volition and doubt (sankalpa and vikalpa) is called Manas the Mind.

The one which stores all experiences and feelings is memory. (chitta).

The entity which feels as "I" and mine and having the character of doer-ship (kartrutva) and enjoyer-ship (Bhoktrutva) is called the Ego.(Ahambhava).

Senses starts functioning only when the mind connects with them.

Biological mind is an instrument, we cannot label it as good or bad.

When it is in the grip of good tendencies it is called good mind, when it is in the grip of bad tendencies it is called a bad mind. Actually the tendencies are either good or bad but not the mind which is an instrument which tendencies use to fulfil and spending up of their desires through the mind.

Action born out of Self-ignorance leads to further action because such action is always incomplete and always leaves the residue of non-understanding. Till we understand the nature of action, the incomplete action born out of Self-ignorance leaves impressions on the mind leading to formation of tendencies which compel us to do further action. This cycle of incomplete action, formation of tendencies, tendencies causing attraction to the objective reality and compelling us to do more action which again is incomplete in its nature is called samsara by Hindus. In complete action done in unawareness in a mechanical way is binding.(Bandha) ,So action must be done in awareness. To do action in awareness mind should not be crowded with too many thoughts and facts which distract the mind attending to the active present. To reduce the thought matter in the mind and to fill it with awareness so that it attends to the active present self-inquiry is the only way. When mind is thus filled with awareness it is disciplined and thought activity is well under control. Such a mind stops volition and doubt. So new tendencies are not born and the old ones die on their own because we no longer give energy to them. Then we are released from the grip of tendencies which is called Moksha. Such a mind undergoes radical transformation which is a real revolution. In physical revolutions mind is not transformed at all and so the same past perpetuates in a new form and so all physical revolutions are bound to fail without exception.

Once we stop volition which is a function of the mind, mind subsides and it becomes one with the pure consciousness.

Mind is a pure witnessor in deep sleep state. (Prajnanaghana) because it disconnects itself from the senses in deep sleep state. It is the senses that recognize the things of objective reality and sends feedback to the mind. So if we can be a witness in the waking mode of mind also there cannot be much thought activity upon which ego feeds itself. We should not forget that any observable entity is not our essential nature. With non-attraction towards the objective reality and doing self-inquiry with earnestness and perseverance mind comes under our control. When rightly used mind helps us to find its source which is Self.

In turning of the mind.(Metanoia, Conversion)

Self-inquiry is the process which helps outgoing mind to turn inward towards its source. Jesus calls this "Metanoia", Christians call conversion.First of all we should stop decorating the ego, then the energy so far utilized in such activity is pooled up which can be utilize to do self-inquiry. Then mind for the first time is endowed with the capacity to see the things "as they really are". Such a mind recognizes the fact that because of the association with Self all the adjuncts are functioning. Then it surrenders itself to the Self. That is real devotion. (Para Bhakti). When the mind recognizes that misery is the outcome of functioning with doer-ship in the objective reality and source of happiness is the inner Self, it never leaves the Self nor it involves in any action which disturbs it from the Self, then a new discipline and a morality depending on sensitivity happens to the mind. In this state we are aware that we have a mind at our disposal but we do not identify with the mind. In this state there is no centre like thinker from which thought arises. There is just free flow of thought-feeling without any obstruction now that there is no obstruction to that flow because there no identity anywhere. It is the identity that blocks the free flow of thoughts, identity is a hindrance to its flow. Once thought-flow is natural and not obstructed thought is not a problem at all. Because of Self-ignorance the Self itself is recognized as the mind. With self-inquiry we recognize that the essence of mind is consciousness and when such understanding happens mind becomes one with the Self.

By doing self-inquiry thought activity is drastically reduced. Though we think of doing so many things what is going to happen will happen. With that understanding we will continue to do the work but we don't give direction to the fruit which is usually the case and which brings misery to us. We must identify the factors which are causing obstruction to the effulgence of Self and making it dormant to lie underneath the deep unconscious layers of the mind. Such factors are just like weeds and removing them is the purpose of self-inquiry and we need not bring the Self anew because it is already the case, the Self is self revealing and self effulgent and no adjunct is needed to know. In fact it is the adjuncts which require the light and energy of Self to reveal their existence. We have to inquire what is that entity which is giving energy that helps the growth of these weeds and there no point in going into details of the weeds and categorize them scientifically. The "self" is continuously giving energy for the weeds to grow. So we are inquiring into the self in self-inquiry. So you are the centre of investigation. The witnessing consciousness helps the mind to subside and at one point there is nothing for that witnessing consciousness for attending to, then it falls back on itself and this falling back causing an implosive state inside releasing enormous energy and bliss. Non-attraction towards the things in the objective reality is dispassion. This comes out of understanding that objective reality is not the source of happiness. Not to leave the source of happiness i. e Self is knowledge. Thoughts are alien to Self and so we should not run after the thoughts and thoughts are possible in metaphysical sleep only. The manifest part of Self always changes and so transient. When the mind superimpose name and form (naam-roop) on Self, it is the Self that appears as creation. Creation is not false but thinking that creation is different from Brahman is a false notion. It is just like thinking that ornament of gold is different from the gold or solid ice floating in deep sea is different from the sea. Because of the action of veiling power of Maya we see Self as the creation. Subsidence of mind means its non-identity with anything. Living without the "me" without its contents, without the feeling of the "mine" ,without tendencies because all these bind the consciousness to non-self and blocks its natural flow. This is called Amanaska yoga which means living with a mind that empty of its contents i. e no-mind state. It is very beautiful if one can live such a life because through such mind "New man" is born who is loving, compassionate, creative, without any ambition and so without any competition and so gone beyond the violence. One should note that body relatives are just accidental. We should know how to live without attachment. Then the mind subsides naturally without being suppressed. Knowing one self will be a total cessation of thinking; it will be simply existing in oneself -- not thinking. Thinking is always about something. Thinking cannot exist in a vacuum, it is always about something. You can think about a chair, you can think about a house, you can think about a friend or an enemy; you cannot think about yourself, because you are! Who is to think? So, if you are to know yourself, you have to cease completely, totally.

The process of thinking must not be there then you are, in your simple authentic existence. Then you are, simply. Then you come to know that mind is not through thinking, that mind is through non-thinking. That's why I define meditation as a state of mind which is not thinking, but is aware -- not thinking and aware. There is no thinking in the mind, but the mind is, and is totally aware. So, about what can it be aware now? There is nothing to think, so it cannot go outside. You can be simply aware. Aware of yourself. You are aware of yourself. But these two things are one -- you and your awareness are not two things. When you are aware of your house, there are two things. But when you are aware of yourself, there is nothing which is aware, and nothing to be aware about -- you are the awareness. Then you are simply awareness. Then you are not aware, you are awareness, because there is only one thing: you and you and you, and awareness -- and nothing to be aware about. This moment, when you are not aware but you are awareness, is meditation. That awareness which is not aware of anything else; it simply exists, like light; it simply exists, like a flame. When awareness becomes objective, when you become aware of something else, then it becomes thinking. Then thinking goes on, thinking is created. When you come subjectively, then there is no possibility of any thinking.

Constant Self awareness(Sada Apramada)

Constant self-awareness helps us to hold onto "Pure-I am-the-body" idea which is not connected to other thoughts. The other thoughts derive energy for their survival from "I-am-the-body" idea and if we hold that mother thought energy to other thoughts is stopped and they die on their own. It is we who cling to those thoughts, tendencies, identities and if we stop giving energy to them in awareness they become weak and gradually they die down. The life span of each and every thought is very short and if we do not give energy to them they die in no time. It is not thoughts that already produced which are the problem but it is the continuous birth of new thoughts which are out of control now is the actual problem. This problem is solved if we can be continuously aware (Sada Apramada). We must recognize that biological mind is the chief sense which helps us to actualize our potential as Self. We must also recognize that if biological mind identifies with the body, beliefs, dogmas, religion, faith, nationality, tendencies, caste, race, color, gender, profession, skill which then becomes the ego, ego is the major obstacle for actualizing our potential as Self because knowingly or unknowing we are so much identified with our ego which is just an utilitarian instrument at our disposal as our Self. Such strong identity with the ego prevents us from investigating into it. When we do action without doer-ship mind does not leave its source even while doing action. Laziness is not inaction but doing work without doer-ship is inaction (Akarma) . Such type of work purifies the mind and a purified mind become eligible for Self knowledge because now it can reflect the Self. Once mind develops the capacity to reflect the Self and tastes the bliss of Self it no longer gives energy to residual tendencies which become very, very weak, finally become extinct and the consciousness so far imprisoned in those tendencies is released from their grip and this release of conscious from tendencies is called Moksha in Vedantic jargon. Such person knows that his essential nature is Pure consciousness and so he just witnesses the events of body-mind complex but never run after them unlike previously.

If we can hold onto to the transitional which happens when mind changes from one mode to another, establishing in the witnessing consciousness is easy and self-inquiry then becomes a cake walk. Then we don't identify with anything and non-identity is the freedom of consciousness

Deliberate inquiry is no inquiry at all. It keeps you in the field of thought, the known. Transformation is possible only outside the field of thought not within it. Real revolution happens outside the field of thought. Real inquiry starts when the mind tastes the unknowable. Such a mind sees the confines, the boundaries of thought and realizes that any change within the field of thought is no change at all. Then such a mind becomes deeper and more extensive and it has the capacity to leave the field of thought and start participating in the unknowable by becoming one with it. This is real surrender, real devotion, real yoga.

Other methods are based on thought that is conditioned

The other methods which are thought based are time bound and they work within the field of known. They help the mind to become eligible to receive the sacred energy by purifying the mind. In Pranayama annihilation of tendencies never happen. The source of violence, greed, jealousy, anger, arrogance, fear, ambition, misery, and desire is the "me". In fact all these combined constitute the "me". So if we keep such me in the name of practicing spiritual discipline how can we get rid of the "me" along with its contents? So self-inquiry in which we remain with the "fact of what is" instead of escaping from it, is the way to get rid of these mental anomalies. Suppose there is anger, if we remain with the anger, is there anger at all? Commonly thought enters and either justifies or condemns the anger and creates an anti-state of anger which is just a mental concept but not an existential entity. In such context there is conflict between the fact of anger and the fictitious anti-anger concept causing inner division. In self-inquiry because thought is bypassed we remain with the fact and the fact dissolves. With the other methods which keep the "me" intact like mantra japa, transcendental meditation, Zen techniques the surface of the mind becomes peaceful, they calm you down initially but no transformation happens inwardly. That surface calm is dangerous because one way or another you will explode again. The inner conflict must be eradicated by dissolving inner division caused by the thought to make you a unitary being. This is possible with self-inquiry because we do self-inquiry with non-comparative observation through witnessing consciousness, also called choice-less awareness and so inner dualistic movement of thought is prevented in the observation of the fact. So if we remain with the fact there is a possibility of delving deep into the Self, but not by escaping from the fact, which is the case in other spiritual methods that retain the "me" for the so called spiritual practices.

Body and soul are not opposite though one is matter and the other is non-matter, They are complimentary to each other. The same current of energy runs in both but at different frequencies and making them look like opposites. They are not divided, they are in deep harmony. They are joined together by the biological mind which contains both matter and consciousness. It ties the consciousness to the matter. (Chit-Jada-Grandhi). The function of the biological mind is to make opposite poles complimentary to each other and to make the life holistic. The food we take definitely has effect on the body-mind complex because both are the products of the food.

Residual impressions and tendencies.

The residual impressions are like heap of straw. You are giving energy to them. With self-inquiry when you know the nature of tendencies and the misery they are causing you no longer give energy to the them. In the fire of Self awareness this heap of impressions are burnt in no time however big the heap may look. Just a spark of fire of Self awareness is enough to burn the whole forest of tendencies and thoughts. This is certain. Even after Self-knowledge the waves of thought continue to be there because just as waves are natural to huge ocean, thoughts are natural to consciousness. They are just dynamic aspect of the consciousness. Moving consciousness is thought. Problem arises only when there is a block in the form of identity to the flow of thoughts then all these thoughts group into a formation around that identity and form as ego and thought forgets its source of sea of Pure consciousness. As long as wave does not forget that it is a part of sea there is no problem. All problems arise because thought waves forget their source and form as the ego and rule the human life as the master without any Self-knowledge. Thought flow happens without the centre of me after gaining Self-knowledge. Mind is a habit. It names, verbalizes whatever it sees, either it may condemn or justify what it perceives, it does not know the art of witnessing, just seeing without verbalizing, condemning, or justifying. When we see outer things we verbalize them, it is a habit of the mind; what a sunset, what beauty is the flight of the bird etc., then perception stops and thinking starts. Similarly we are incapable of seeing the inner conflict in us without either condemning it or justifying it mainly due to the result oriented attitude of the mind. The result oriented mind is a stupid mind because it is in stupor, it cannot see, perceive things "as they are" as a witness. When there is an end to be gained there is no possibility of pure seeing, either there is condemnation or justification. Pure seeing is simple. When there is an end to be gained during the observation, there is a direction given to the seeing and that direction limits the seeing, duality and so conflict are created. So self-inquiry done with an end to be gained is always painful and arduous but simple awareness of conflict with witnessing attitude is simple. Seeing transforms the mind, seeing itself is action, there is no other end to be gained. So we must be aware that thought contaminates and increases conflict if it is allowed to function during self-inquiry. When we relate to the existence or to others we are not aware of what is going on in the inner subject; like conflict, condemnation, approval or denial, struggle, futility, despair, hope, frustration. If we don't see the operations of the mind like these totally, it implies that we are not totally aware. Unawareness is always punished in the form of perennial misery; awareness is rewarded immediately without any time gap with bliss that is inherent to the released energy from the contents of the mind. In self-inquiry we mainly attend to the subject, the ego, it becomes the object of observation by the witnessing consciousness. The subject i.e. ego is full of rubbish with various forms of identities. With the light of awareness, these identities are gone, non-essential is gone and the essential asserts itself spontaneously. Once the rubbish of ego is dropped, the ultimate reality will reveal itself spontaneously. Then you have come home.

Tendencies are products of evolution. Human has animal inheritance. That is why human is violent by birth. The unconscious layers of the mind are the store house of tendencies. All the tendencies have to be spent before consciousness in them is released. Human birth is for spending up of tendencies. We can spend them consciously also then such type of tendency never takes roots in the unconscious past. In self-inquiry though there may be thought flow it will never take roots in the unconscious layers because in self-inquiry everything is done in awareness. The entity which feels that he is a sinner is ego. When we do action with doer-ship and enjoyer-ship such thoughts occur to us. Till these concepts of doer-ship and enjoyer-ship are annihilated through understanding we must continue to do self-inquiry. We should not stop self-inquiry just by tasting the Self once. It must be continued till all tendencies get annihilated and we are firmly established as the Pure conscious being. By doing action without doer-ship gradually identity with the gross body is dissolved. With devotion identity with the subtle body is lost. With Self knowledge identity with the causal body is annihilated. The very meaning of the word Deha (body) means that which can be burnt. In this way the three bodies are purified and through these Purified bodies Pure consciousness and though-feeling flow unobstructed. This is the state of Jnani (Self realized soul with the body). Tendencies belonging to five sheaths of the body are blocks to the free flow of consciousness. They filter the consciousness just as clouds filter the light of the Sun. When we say destruction of five sheaths of body it is not literal destruction but it indicates that we no longer identify with those sheaths. For attaining this non-identity with the bodies we have to do self-inquiry with earnestness, just be as a witness to the events in the phenomenal reality.

Annihilation of tendencies (Vasana Kshaya)

Till all tendencies get annihilated we have to do self-inquiry. We must always be aware while we are doing so that it does not leave any impression on the mind. Action done in unawareness definitely leave impression on the mind, when done repeatedly and mechanically like that it becomes a habit and finally leads to formation of new tendencies. We must take care that new tendencies are not formed and we should not give energy to the old tendencies. Whatever we do we must do without any doer-ship, then new tendencies are never formed because there is no intention behind that work. Losing the identity with the non-Self amounts to gaining the Self. Ego life is possible only in unawareness. Once we bring in the light of awareness, ego and the things associated with it disappear and only the Self remains. Pure consciousness is the basis of everything and underlies as the witness of all events that happen. The one who is free of identity with the non-Self is said to be born in Self. Such person is called Dwija which means twice born, one is the physical birth and another is birth in the Self. Dwija-hood is not a heritable entity, though some castes in India claim like that. Earnest self-inquiry helps the consciousness to grow into a huge tree that can give shelter to others also by breaking the shell of conditioning which is hindering the growth of consciousness. Events in the phenomenal reality cannot move such a person just like water flow of a stream cannot move a mountain. Disconnecting with the past in awareness is self-inquiry. Whenever we are disconnected with the past we are joyful in daily life. Children live in the present moment and they are joyful because they are not bothered about the events of the past. That is the meaning when Jesus says unless you become child-like you cannot enter the kingdom of god. We cannot dry up water with the help of water. We cannot annihilate thought through thought. That is the meaning when JK says analysis of mind is useless because in analysis thought is used. The observer and the observed are both conditioned entities and such inquiry is a deliberate inquiry. Deliberate inquiry keeps us within the limits of thought and the known and no transformation is possible if we use thought in self-inquiry. Transformation is possible when we go beyond the thought into the timeless and limitless sky of consciousness whose basic nature is bliss. Unfortunately all the western philosophy and all the religions are thought base and so no transformation of human is possible through these thought based things. It is quite obvious that all religions have failed in solving human problem. That is why Bhagawan chose self-inquiry to deliver the goods. In self-inquiry mind dives into spiritual heart and enjoys the bliss of it. But only an empty which is free of contents can dive into spiritual heart. So at any cost we must get rid of the contents of the mind if we are interested to taste the bliss of spiritual heart. If we have strong longing for the bliss, the contents of the mind emptied through self-inquiry quickly. As long as we feel we are the "I" thought it continues to rise and subsides in a cyclical fashion. But if we can posit in thought-free state of being, the consciousness shines with splendor. Because of god's grace only we start doing self-inquiry and explore our inner self. In the initial stages effort is needed to dive into the inner but when mind is pure and so mature the inner Self draws the mind like a magnet pulling the iron filing, then no effort is needed and actually effort is a hindrance in that context. If we offer ego to Self it is a real offering and real devotion and surrender. Such complete surrender is possible only with god's grace. The action of grace will not happen to lazy people. The action of grace happens only to earnest truth seekers. For earnest truth seekers the bliss of sleep happens in the waking mode of mind also. If during self-inquiry doubts arise note that mind has entered into the inquiry to spoil it. Just as dog identifies its master through his smell, we can identify our master i. e Self if we hold on to the "Pure I-am-the-body idea." Bhagawan says The word "diving" is appropriate when there are outgoing tendencies, and when, therefore, the mind has to be directed and turned within, there is a dip below the surface externalities. But when quietness prevails without obstructing the Consciousness, where is the need to dive?

The Nature of the Mind.

Mind is consciousness in movement; when that movement stops "minding" *(thinking)* stops. To illustrate, suppose that we engage in walking and stop, the legs are still there but the process, the function of walking has stopped. Likewise, when pedaling a bicycle; as long as you pedal the bicycle moves, if you stop pedaling it stops moving but the bicycle will still be there. So when minding (*thinking*) stops consciousness remains as a silent pool of energy. You are that consciousness. Minding (*thinking*) is a function of consciousness but your nature is not the minding *(thinking)*. The nature of minding is movement. If that movement is stopped for any reason then there is no such thing as mind. Thought is the mind. so If there is stilling of thought for any reason then there is no entity as mind (*naiva manasam*). In such a state we encounter a static aspect of consciousness with full senses. The nature of such static consciousness is existence, Self-knowledge (*awareness*), bliss (*tranquility, peace*).

Identity with the mind.

You think you are the mind. This fallacious idea that you are the mind gives the mind total freedom, because then there is no one to master it, to control it. There is no one! Mind itself becomes the master, but that mastery is just seemingly so. Try once and you can break that mastery – it is false. This breaking up of the process of minding is possible in self-inquiry. Then you will find out for yourself the nature of the static aspect of consciousness and the nature of the minding which is just the dynamic function of consciousness. There is nothing wrong in minding but identifying with that minding and believing that the minding is the "me" (*thinker*) is the wrong state of affairs. Then we go on minding whether it is required or not. In self-inquiry that pathological minding stop and we develop mastery over the minding. If we master the minding, then the mind is one of our best servants. But at present the mind is behaving like a master without any control bringing so much disaster, disorder, chaos to the individual and society at large. Through self-inquiry we develop the capacity to allow minding when it is necessary and stop minding where it has no role to play. For example thought i.e. mind has no role to play in human relations but we relate with each other through thought only which definitely brings conflict and strife to the relationship. So, if we can situate ourselves in the static aspect of consciousness when relating with another, then the relating is based on the present moment and we will have a healthy relationship.

In science and technology we require minding and we should allow minding there. Once that task is over minding should stop and we should be back to our natural centre of static aspect of consciousness and enjoy the serenity, tranquility, peace and bliss of it. This is possible through self-inquiry. Then we become the master of our own mind which is superior to being emperor of the whole world. Existence feels fulfilled through us by becoming master of the mind. This is the purpose for which we are born on earth but we are preoccupied with doing all sorts of silly things which takes us to the present state of our highly disordered life.

Creation is the clothing of Brahman.

In the "presence" of pure consciousness creation happens through self-ignorance. Just in the light of the ultimate all creation happens without any desire on the part of ultimate. This is the meaning of word "Meenakshi". It means creation happens just by her look. God, world, Individual consciousness are part of this self-ignorant activity. Creation means happening of the world of name and form. Self-ignorance is the power of Self. Self-ignorant Maya is like clothing to the Brahman. So the same Brahman i. e Self with the help of its power manifests as multiplicity. Brahman pervades every atom in this cosmos. The purpose of creation is to release this imprisoned consciousness. So what exists is only Self and everything is the work of Self in the ultimate analysis.

Surrender

Many feel that surrender makes us dependent on the master or god to whom we surrender. On the contrary for the first time we become independent and dignified individual if our surrender is real and total. (Poorna Saranagathi). Actually we are surrendering that which never existed in real terms. You cannot surrender that which you really are. Ego is your bogus existence, bogus individuality, ego is just a combination of many fragments, so it is pseudo-individuality, a pretender, counterfeit, it is not our real thing. So when we surrender the ego we become "that which we really are" and our real existence as pure consciousness is not dependent, it is self-sustaining, self-effulgent, it reveals itself without the aid of any other entity. So surrender makes you independent as nothing else can make you. During death experience when sudden unaccounted for fear gripped Bhagawan he surrendered to existence and inquired into the entity which feels it is dying and he became enlightened in just 20 minutes. Such a thing was never heard of in spiritual history. Basically he is a heart oriented person having complete trust in existence which many call as god. When devotees asked his advise in spiritual matters his first priority is to advise them to surrender to the existence though he is well renowned for his self-inquiry method for self-realization. He advised self-inquiry method which by passes head and thought to those whose consciousness is fully centered in head and whose nature is to argue and reason rather than trust. He never advised analysis in the name of self-inquiry.

- By surrendering you become independent because in surrender you disappear as ego consciously, when you as ego disappear, boundaries, limitations, definitions imposed on you by you and the society in the form of conditioning disappear and you as a consciousness melt and merge with the universal conscious existence and you become holy in the sense that you become one with the whole. A mystic is one who becomes one with the existence forever.

- By surrendering to a master like Bhagawan, in a way you are not surrendering to anybody, because in reality Bhagawan is a nobody because there is not even a trace of ego left in him. So for all practical purposes if you say that you are surrendering to Bhagawan, you are surrendering to a great nothingness, i.e. Paramatman. After attaining certain maturity in life, when the mind ripens, we want some pretext or the other to surrender and so we decide to surrender to a master whom we like because we are very much impressed and influenced by great qualities that the master has, his profound teachings which paves the way for Self realization, we say "I have surrendered my ego to such and such a master". It is just a plea, we cannot help but surrendering to the whole in some name or the other. In reality you are surrendering to great nothingness whose nature is oneness. Naming that nothingness after a master's name is a habit of human naming everything it encounters whether it knows the nature of the entity which it names or not is a different matter. Unless it names human mind is restless and fearful.

It is an attempt of the mind to name the unnamable and unknowable in the language of the known.

- Mind is basically afraid of the unknowable because it does not know how to deal with the vast unknowable, mind is too petty for that purpose, so it becomes satisfied by naming the unknowable.

By surrendering to that great nothingness, we pass through it and come to our own being.

Master is an embodiment of that great nothingness and so we can pass through the nothingness of the one we know and trust and come to our own being finally. So master helps us by being our passage. Plunging of our mind in the great nothingness of the master is easy and it happens without any effort on our part and plunging into his nothingness amounts to plunging into our own nothingness (Atma Samsthithi of the mind) because there can be only one nothingness in the universe.

- Dependency has nothing to do with surrender. If surrender becomes a dependency, know well that you have not surrendered to nothingness (Shunyata, Paramatman), you are deceiving yourself in the name of surrender, you have missed the beauty of independence of surrender. If you still feel psychologically dependent even after surrender, know that ego is playing a game with you in the name of surrender, on one hand it says "I am surrendered" but it is very much there.

- When you are really surrendered, there is nobody to say "I am surrendered". Nothing is left except the clarity of witnessing consciousness, choice-less awareness; a transparency of vision is all that there is, after real total surrender (Sampoorna Saranagathi). Then you have clear vision devoid of layers of conditioning and you perceive things "as they really are" and you don't project anything on them because, the entity which projects i.e. the ego is surrendered and no longer interferes or distorts the perception. You act out of awareness moment to moment, you don't try to manipulate "what is", you don't try to control your life anymore. You always live in a "let go" mood and to respond to challenge in the present moment spontaneously without the shadow and burden of the past.

- Ego's way to deal with life is to manage, to control, to plan, to carry decisions from the past. This way is good when we deal with the physical things in the phenomenal reality. Progress in the outer world is possible through such approach. But we are applying the same technique in the psychological world where we deal with psychological things which demand passive awareness in the stillness of mind but not control, manipulate, manage, decisions based on past experiences which complicates an already disordered mind. Managing, manipulating psychological things and problems increase mental activity and perpetuate the past. That is what everybody is doing and everybody is creating hell out of life. This is quite obvious.

- We cannot solve the psychological problems like anger, greed, violence, ambition, jealousy with its competition, relationship problems which are primarily born out when we act from our past memory of relationship through control, suppression, manipulation, planning. We have to inquire into them with passive awareness of still mind. The way of surrender is the enlightened way of life in which we have no private goals to achieve, not to carry any plan or decision based on the past to fulfill those self projected private goals, but to wait for the moment of challenge to come and to respond to that challenge from the totality of consciousness not fearing about consequences of such response.

- So once you surrender the fragmentary and limited ego, you become one with the totality of witnessing consciousness. When you surrender the ego you surrender your plans, your past, and your projected future. Now emptiness which is full with consciousness and bliss is left behind and you act from that content-less consciousness of the empty mind. Action from that empty mind is total action because you are acting from the totality of the consciousness. Action from the ego is partial and fragmentary and so action born out of the ego always leads to conflict.

- So if anybody feels dependent psychologically after surrender, he missed the essence of surrender and he is crippled. If we imitate the master or look at the master for help for every minor thing that happens in life it indicates that we have not opened our mental eye and so we are blind and paralyzed. We have to learn from the masters but we should not ignore the uniqueness gifted to us by the existence. We must remain open and vulnerable. It needs great sensitivity to surrender. You can surrender yet you can remain as your natural uniqueness. It sounds paradoxical but in that very paradox there is beauty and benediction, dignity of surrender.

- I have gone through life stories of many, many great masters from east and west. I read life stories of all Nayanars, Alwars, Upanishadic seers, Buddha, all recent mystics but i am surprised at the level of surrender Bhagawan has. Starting from his death experience which led to his enlightenment, then his holy pilgrimage to Arunachala, not signing the letter written to his brother indicating that he is none other than that great nothingness we call as Paramatman, Darshan of Arunachaleswara in big temple submitting himself fully to lord saying "Appa (father), I have come here at your command, this upadhi (his body) is yours, you use it as you please". He faced so much inconvenience in the early days of his stay at Arunachala, just taking whatever aaku kurala avva used to provide him as food, living in Virupaksha cave and Skandasram, coming down to hill near his mother's samadhi to confer self-knowledge to some and clearing genuine doubts of many, remaining unmoved when some anti-social elements tried to destroy both his eyes, no planning anything in life, the way he took the deadly disease of sarcoma of left arm of his body so lightly, his adoration of Arunachaleswara in Akshara Mana Malai and Arunachala stuti panchakam etc. All these show unparalleled complete surrender (Poorna Saranagathi). Because he taught self-inquiry many feel that his way is only Jnana marga. But to me he is an embodiment of love and surrender; his Jnana and Para Bhakti are born out of them. That is why when he left the body he raised like a blue colour meteor which happened only in case of Lord Krishna. So let us surrender to Bhagawan who is none other than Paramatman (great nothingness fully filled with consciousness and bliss) and enjoy the beauty, glory, independent, enlightened surrendered way of life.

Importance of self-inquiry

Ego is a product of evolution. At present we are slaves to the ego and the result is perennial misery. self-Inquiry is the alchemy of transformation from this state of slavery to the mastery of mind mechanism. It shatters all chains and hindrances which are the result of identity to the body-mind complex, beliefs, dogmas, nationality, religion, race, caste, creed, erudition, etc. which are interfering for Self to be spontaneously revealed. They are hovering over the Sun of Self and obstructing its flow of light. If we are watchful, aware, Self recollected, we utilize every experience and thought as a means to guide us towards the Self. In self-inquiry there is continual conquering of inner cravings, passions, hopes, despairs, vain pursuits, desire to be consoled and comforted by understanding all these. Once we understand them, there is wearing down of all these, resulting in consciousness liberated from all these limiting factors that were produced during the process of evolution. Pure consciousness is the background, the screen on which all these limiting factors are painted during evolution. That screen is the dwelling place of pure intuition, of pure action. When something is placed before that dwelling place, it always gives a right response.

But nobody wants to change, change needs effort and the average human is borne lazy. Change means going into the unknown and men are cowards. Though everybody knows that known is nothing but misery, still they cling to it because they prefer the known devil than an unknown angel. Through self-inquiry we reach pure being, there is cessation of effort, then we live by pure intuition, pure seeing, pure perception without the interference of past in the form of thought.

So in self-inquiry we become our own liberators. So let us do self-inquiry and get liberated from all limitations which are a product of evolution and which apparently are limiting our consciousness and giving a false notion of separate existence from the whole.

Any being without Self-knowledge identifies with the body-mind complex. As far as life in the outside world is concerned "I" thought i.e. ego has certain utilitarian value and without the "I" thought life in the world becomes impossible. Bhagawan said even Jnanis have "I" thought but they use it like an instrument for the welfare of the world but they never, under any circumstances, identify themselves with the "I" thought and they are always attuned to their essential nature of pure consciousness. But when common man says "I" he is referring to the body-mind complex as "I" because he is identified with them. Once a great German philosopher came back to his house and placed his umbrella on his bed and he stood in the corner where he used to keep his umbrella usually. This is because he mistook the umbrella for himself on that day and he is in the position of the umbrella mistaking his own body as the umbrella. Only in the early hours he recognized this wrong identity and then behaved normally. The position of the whole humanity is in a similar context of mistaken identity. They are identifying with the utilities of the body and mind as their essential nature and they completely forgot their essential nature and so their life is topsy turvy, believing the false as real. They must realize that utilities are not realities. Life is short and energy is limited and we are not expected to go on wasting in utilities which are not our essentials. Only when we are conscious and come to the understanding that the utilities are just instruments in the hands of our essential pure consciousness, only then we develop the capacity to drop them. This is real renunciation but not changing physical circumstances, or renouncing the physical things which is relatively easy nor leading a sado-masochist life in the name of religion to attract the attention of others. The word religion literally means to gather energy available to us to prevent the utilities to superimpose their activities on our essential pure consciousness. The quality of the mind which perceives the reality beyond thought is religiosity. Religiosity does not mean belonging to an organized religion, belief or dogma. Only when the identity to the nonessential utilities is dropped, only then there is a possibility to get attuned with the essential. Seeing the false as false is the beginning of seeing the true as true. Thought has a role to play in the life of the physical world and it can solve some physical problems. We are using the same instrument of thought for solving the psychological problems also, which are the result of thought interference in the psychological arena where it has no role to play. Thought is a response of memory and memory being limited, the action of thought is always limited, leaving the residue of non-understanding resulting in conflict and strife. The same thought is also trying to manipulate and correct these anomalies of conflict and strife which is impossible for thought to solve. When there is a psychological problem we must attend to it and to pay attention one must be quiet without the noise of thought. The problem must be given an opportunity to unfold itself and so give its full significance in the passive awareness of attention. First of all we must learn watching. What you watch is not important, it may be a song or a flight of a bird, clouds, sky, the flow of a river, falling of old leaves, watching the breath or walking with awareness and in these situations thought has no role to play so set aside. We are so accustomed to occupation with thought that we feel more comfortable when we are occupied. Just test for yourself by sitting with your eyes closed there starts inner chattering in a crazy way, relevant and irrelevant thoughts criss cross your being, nothing seems to happen except a very long procession of thoughts, desires, memories and they go on coming unendingly. Watchfulness is the right antidote for this. When watchfulness crosses a break-even point, thought traffic stops and the outer shell of the mind i.e. thoughts drop and when there is nothing else to be attended to, awareness falls on itself and for the first time you know yourself. When you lose your personality which is a conditioning imposed on you by the society through self-inquiry, you gain your natural state of pure consciousness. So watchfulness is the method of destroying the identity with utilities like ego and the body, and self-inquiry is nothing but a passive state of watchfulness of ego activities in which ego is given an opportunity to unfold itself and wither. So let us do self-inquiry to destroy the identity with the utilities of body and mind and establish ourselves in the source of them which is adjunct less , thought-free, basic pure consciousness "I am". In self-inquiry the rust of the past is taken away and the seed of light which is in the depths of the mind (reflected consciousness, Abhasa, Jiva) breaks open the ground and becomes one with its source. The whole existence supports and celebrates if the flame and fire of the quest of "who am i" pierces through and moves within the spiritual heart and so the genuine quest, thirst for truth is in the heart but not in the head. self-inquiry is a journey from head to heart, from periphery to the centre, from trivia of utilities to the essential, from ignorance to truth.

Waking state is a wonderful opportunity for self-inquiry.

Though in the metaphysical sense the waking mode is also a dream, the waking mod is the right mode of mind to do self-inquiry. Certain events in ordinary dream make us to wake up. Similarly doing self-inquiry and association of a Self realized master help us to awake into the Self from this long metaphysical sleep. The substratum Self is appearing as waking mode of mind and this is an opportunity to have a close look at that mode and realize it as none other than the Self. Actually looking at the events in the waking mode we develop dispassion and if we are watchful to al the events we will be free from the imposed conditioning. I feel that waking mode is a god given opportunity for doing self-inquiry and instead wasting life by indulging in trivia better we do self-inquiry and actualize our potential as the Self.

In the initial stages of quest for truth scriptures give us an idea of our essential being and point us that truth is in the inner. They help us to discriminate what is false and what is true and it is up to us to know them existentially. Self-inquiry is not an acquisitive process of accumulating scriptural information and on the contrary it is a de-learning process and destroys the structures built by the thought. So too much indulgence in scriptures leads to tendency of accumulating of scriptural information on which thought again builds up new structures. A great person like Sri Ganapathi Sastry who is respected by Bhagawan and is very close to him could not come out of this habit of scriptural learning. So we must be careful about this trap of this learning and consequent respectability associated with it. Many fall into this trap.

Role of scriptural knowledge.

Bhagawan never advised accumulation of information in the name of spirituality. His method is self-inquiry which is a process of de-learning and throwing contents of the mind through understanding. Every other spiritual methods require the "me" to do it. Majority of spiritual techniques involve doing in some form or the other. But Realization of Self is not an outcome of any "doing". In self-inquiry we don't depend on the "me" and on the contrary we question the very integrity of the "me". So a serious seeker of self-inquiry does not indulge in accumulation of information in the name of spirituality. But average devotee cannot help but reading some spiritual books. Bhagawan advised Rubhu Gita,Yoga Vasistam,Kaivalya Navaneetam and Tripura Rahasya.I have gone through all these books and Rhubhu gita is fully devoted to self-inquiry,Kaivalya Navaneetam and Tripura Rahasya are extremely useful in deepening our understanding in self-inquiry. Unlike them Yoga Vasista is not fully devoted to self-inquiry because it conveys Vedanta in story form. That is their way of presentation. But Vasista allotted 300 pages fully to highlight the importance of self-inquiry if one want to get released from body identity, identity to dogmas and beliefs, caste, race, nationality, family, gender, profession, wealth etc. It is quite surprising that genius of India opted to inquire into the self rather than running for material gains. In this book what is said in Yoga vasista about self-inquiry is being conveyed. He himself wrote Akshara Mana Malai, Upadesa saram, Ulladu Narpadu, Unnadi Nalubadi Sadvidya , Arunachala Pancha Ratnam, commentary on Viveka Chudamani of Adi Sankara, etc for the benefit of understanding of devotees.

Pleasure is different from bliss.

The word happiness depends upon the state of consciousness we are in. If we are metaphysically asleep which is usually the case we use the word happiness for pleasure. Pleasure is a sensation trying to achieve through the body-mind complex which is not possible through it but forcing to achieve through it. That complex can give you only momentary pleasures and is balanced by equal amount of pain. your pain will be followed by pleasure.

But you will never be at ease. When you will be in a state of pleasure you will be afraid that you are going to lose it, and that fear will poison it. And when you will be lost in pain, of course, you will be in suffering, and you will try every possible effort to get out of it -- just to fall again back into it. Sometimes pleasure comes up and sometimes pain comes up, but we are crushed between these two rocks. whatsoever you call pleasure is, at the most, just a relief of a tense state. Sexual energy gathers, accumulates; you become tense and heavy and you want to release it.

The man who is asleep, his sexuality is nothing but a relief, like a good sneeze. It gives you nothing but a certain relief. A tension was there, now it is no more there; but it will accumulate again. Food gives you only a little taste on the tongue; it is not much to live for. But many people are living only to eat; But this is the world of pleasure. The dog can be forgiven, but you cannot be forgiven. To the sleeping, pleasurable sensations are happiness. He lives from one pleasure to another pleasure. He is just rushing from one sensation to another sensation. He lives for small thrills. His life is very superficial; it has no depth, it has no quality. He lives in the world of quantity.

Then the people who are in between, who are neither asleep nor awake, who are just in a limbo, a little bit asleep, a little bit awake. You sometimes have that experience in the early morning: still sleepy, but you can't say you are asleep. This is the transitional state, Bija Jagrat.

The same happens when you start meditating. The non-meditator sleeps, dreams; the meditator starts moving away from his sleep towards awakening. He is in a transitory state. Then happiness has a totally different meaning: it becomes more of a quality, less of a quantity; it is more psychological, less physiological. He enjoys music more, he enjoys poetry more, he enjoys creating something. He enjoys nature, its beauty. He enjoys silence. He enjoys what he had never enjoyed before, and this is far more lasting. Even if the music stops, something goes on lingering in you. And it is not a relief.

The difference between pleasure and bliss is, it is not a relief, it is an enrichment. You become more full, you become a little overflowing. Listening to good music, something is triggered in your being, a harmony arises in you—you become musical. Or dancing, suddenly you forget your body; your body becomes weightless. The grip of gravitation over you is lost. Suddenly you are in a different space: the ego is not so solid, the dancer melts and merges into the dance. This is far higher, far deeper than the joy that you gain from food or sex. This has a depth. But this is also not the ultimate.

The ultimate happens only when you are fully awake, when you are a Buddha like Bhagawan, when all sleep is gone and all dreaming is gone, when your whole being is full of light, when there is no darkness within you. All darkness has disappeared and with that darkness, the ego is gone. All tensions have disappeared, all anguish, all anxiety. You are in a state of total contentment. You live in the present; no past, no future anymore. You are utterly here-now.

This moment is all. Now is the only time and here is the only space. And then suddenly the whole sky drops into you. This is bliss. This is real happiness.

This moment is all. Now is the only time and here is the only space. And then suddenly the whole sky drops into you. This is bliss. This is real happiness.

Seek bliss, through self-inquiry, it is your birthright. Don't remain lost in the jungle of pleasures; rise a little higher. Reach to happiness and then to bliss.

Pleasure is animal, happiness is human, bliss is divine. Pleasure binds you, it is a bondage, it chains you. Happiness gives you a little more rope, a little bit of freedom, but only a little bit. Bliss is absolute freedom. You start moving upwards; it gives you wings. You are no more part of the gross earth; you become part of the sky. You become light, you become joy.

Pleasure is dependent on others. Happiness is not so dependent on others, but still it is separate from you. Bliss is not dependent, is not separate either; it is your very being; it is your very nature. To attain it is to attain to God, to nirvana.

Watchfulness-Self-inquiry

The mind cannot do self-inquiry, because whatsoever the mind does will strengthen it. Any doing on the part of the mind makes the mind stronger. So self-inquiry by the mind is impossible. Mind doing something means mind perpetuating itself and that is not in the nature of things. But self-inquiry happens through watching the mind, not by doing anything.

The watcher is separate from the mind; it is deeper than the mind, higher than the mind. The watcher is always hidden behind the mind. A thought passes, a feeling arises — who is watching this thought? Not the mind itself — because mind is nothing but the process of thought and feeling. The mind is just the traffic of thinking. Who is watching it? When you say, "Fear has arisen in me," who are 'you'? To whom has the thought of fear arisen? Who is the container? The thought of fear is the content — who is the container?

Consciousness (awareness) is like an empty paper. Mind is like a written, printed paper. Whatever exists as an object inside you, whatever you can see and observe, is the mind. The perceiver is not the mind, the observed is the mind. So if you can simply go on observing, watching, witnessing without condemning, without in any way creating a conflict with the mind, without indulging it, without following it, without going against it, if you can simply be there indifferent to it, in that indifference self-inquiry happens; when the watcher arises, the witness is there, mind simply disappears.

Mind exists with your cooperation or your opposition. Both are ways of cooperating — opposition too! When you fight with the mind, you give energy to it. If you really fight you have accepted the mind, in your very fighting you have established the power of the mind over your being. So whether you cooperate or you oppose, in both cases the mind becomes stronger and stronger. Just watch. Just be a witness. And, by and by, you will see gaps arising. A thought passes, and another thought does not come immediately — there is an interval. In that interval is peace. In that interval is love. In that interval is all that you always seek — but never find. In that gap, you are no longer an ego. In that gap you are not defined, confined, imprisoned. In that gap you are vast, immense, huge! In that gap you are one with existence — the barrier does not exist. Your boundaries are not there any longer. You melt into existence and the existence melts in you. You start overlapping. This happens if you go on watching without getting attached to these gaps either… because that is our nature, to get attached to these gaps. If you start yearning for these gaps… because they are tremendously beautiful, they are immensely blissful and it is natural to get attached to them, and desire arises to have more and more of these gaps — then you will miss them, then your watcher has disappeared. In that way those gaps will again disappear, and again the traffic of the mind will be there. So the first thing is to become an indifferent watcher. And the second thing is to remember that when beautiful gaps arise, don't get attached to them, don't start asking for them, don't start waiting for them to happen more often. If you can remember these two things — when beautiful gaps come, watch them too, and keep your indifference alive — then one day the traffic simply disappears with the road, they both disappear. And there is tremendous emptiness. That's what Buddha calls 'Nirvana' — the mind has ceased. This is what I call suicide — but mind has not committed it. Mind cannot do it. You can help it to happen or you can hinder it; helping it to happen depends on you, not on your mind. Anything the mind does will always strengthen the mind. So self-inquiry is not really an effort of the mind. Real meditation is not effort at all.

Real self-inquiry (Nija Vicharana) is just allowing the mind to have its own way, and not interfere in any way whatsoever — just remain watchful, witnessing. It silences, by and by, it becomes still. One day it is gone. You are left alone. That aloneness is what your reality is. And reality is beginning less and endless. The mind has a beginning and an end, hence the mind and reality cannot meet. The mind cannot comprehend the eternal. Reality is simply the loss of ego. Destroy the ego by seeking its identity. Because the ego is no entity it will automatically vanish and reality will shine forth by itself. And in that aloneness nothing is excluded, remember it. In that aloneness everything is included — that aloneness is God. That purity, that innocence, uncorrupted by any thought, is what Self is.

Self-inquiry drives the Divine Spark in Ego Back to its Source

Every time we arise from sleep, a conscious spark, pure ego (Visphulingam) from pure awareness identifies itself with tendencies, personality of the individual and gets enmeshed in them and forgets its source from where it has come, feels separate from the rest of existence including its source. The mind is always burdened with the memories of the past and projections of the future causing a lot of thought traffic which cause the clouding of the light of this spark. The mind has the inherent power to create illusions and tempt this spark to get distracted. So this power of the mind to create illusions, its mechanics of functioning must be understood before thought-feeling can be wholly separated free from its own self created distractions.

If one begins to be aware of the outer distractions like possessions, relationships, amusements, pleasures, addictions with drugs or sex, we can trace that the cause of the outer distraction actually is in the inner. The inner distractions are an escape from the facts, like ambition, greed, violence, anger, fear, arrogance etc. and they are substituted by the acquisition of knowledge, competitiveness possessiveness, speculative curiosity, self-protective beliefs, psychiatric dogmas, memories etc. These are discovered when there is awareness of the outer and inner distractions at the same time. The Pathology of distraction is not knowing the source of the spark. With awareness of self-inquiry there is deep understanding that thought-feeling, which in itself has become a means of its own escape, is its own cause of ignorance. As understanding and awareness deepens, we drop unnecessary thoughts, the dust we have collected from centuries and then this divine spark of consciousness appears clean, clear, alive, and young. Then our whole life becomes aflame without any smoke. So in self-inquiry we isolate this divine conscious spark from its association with the jungle of distractions both outer and inner. Every human is endowed with this divine spark and if we can develop our own methodology to isolate it from association with the non-essential, this spark shows us the way to reach our life source which is also the universal source. In this way the spark which is the essence of the individual disentangles itself from distractions naturally, easily, effortlessly and the spark unites with its source and understands that it is never left its source though for centuries it felt separate from it. This understanding is the fruit of doing self-inquiry. Meditation is our natural state of being.

Uncovering the ultimate reality.

Self-Inquiry is the process of uncovering the ultimate reality which is apparently clouded by thoughts. We cannot investigate into the Self. It is a process of negating thought clouds which are causing apparent clouding of consciousness and preventing us from seeing things "as they really are". Self is oneness and a unitary whole. The ignorant mind cannot investigate into the self. It is enough if we set aside the ignorant mind so that Self is uncovered; self-inquiry is not a search for truth. The search for truth is merely a fulfillment of belief. self-Inquiry is the process of understanding how thought works and the nature of the thinker. It explores what the thinker is and his thoughts. Without understanding this self isolation process which we commonly call the "thinker or ego" the ultimate reality is not uncovered. Merely getting caught in a dogma is not uncovering the beauty of Self which is life, existence, truth.

Conserving energy to do self-inquiry.

Self-inquiry demands psychological energy. But the energy is destroyed, is wasted when one is in conflict. So when there is the understanding of the whole process of conflict, there is the ending of conflict, there is abundance of energy. Then you can proceed, tearing down the house that you have built throughout the centuries and that has no meaning at all. You know, to destroy is to create. We must destroy the psychological, the unconscious and the conscious defences, securities that one has built up rationally, individually, deeply, and superficially. We must tear through all that to be utterly defense-less, because you must be defenceless to love and have affection. Then you see and understand ambition, authority; and you begin to see when authority is necessary and at what level -the authority of the policeman and no more. Then there is no authority of learning, no authority of knowledge, no authority of capacity, no authority that function assumes and which becomes status. To understand all authority -of the gurus, of the Masters, and others- requires a very sharp mind, a clear brain, not a muddy brain, not a dull brain.

The word "diving" is appropriate when there are outgoing tendencies, and when, therefore, the mind has to be directed and turned within, there is a dip below the surface externalities. But when quietness prevails without obstructing the Consciousness, where is the need to dive?

Self-ignorance to Self knowledge.(Tamasoma Jyotirgamaya)

Humanity is in dark state of Self-ignorance. Ego is a product of this Self-ignorant dark state and the god, religion, poetry, art, painting it creates are all outcome of this darkness. The culture of human society, its education, family system, beliefs, dogmas all add to this metaphysical sleep and keeps the human in darkness causing lot of misery to him. Because ego state is a dark state we have to bring in light of "awareness" to know how the ego is working and causing suffering to humanity. For this self-inquiry is the direct method and this book deals with that study of self. Self-inquiry demands psychological energy. But the energy is destroyed, is wasted when one is in conflict. So when there is the understanding of the whole process of conflict, there is the ending of conflict, there is abundance of energy. Then you can proceed, tearing down the house that you have built throughout the centuries and that has no meaning at all. You know, to destroy is to create. We must destroy the psychological, the unconscious and the conscious defences, securities that one has built up rationally, individually, deeply, and superficially. We must tear through all that to be utterly defence-less, because you must be defence less to love and have affection. Then you see and understand ambition, authority; and you begin to see when authority is necessary and at what level -the authority of the policeman and no more. Then there is no authority of learning, no authority of knowledge, no authority of capacity, no authority that function assumes and which becomes status. To understand all authority -of the gurus, of the Masters, and others- requires a very sharp mind, a clear brain, not a muddy brain, not a dull brain. Is there an action not of desire? If we ask such a question, and we rarely do, one can probe, without any motive, to find an action which is of intelligence. The action of desire is not intelligent; it leads to all kinds of problems and issues. Is there an action of intelligence? One must always be somewhat skeptical in these matters; doubt is an extraordinary factor of purification of the brain, of the heart. Doubt, carefully measured out, brings great clarity, freedom. In the Eastern religions, to doubt, to question, is one of the necessities for finding truth, but in the religious culture of Western civilization, doubt is an abomination of the devil. But in freedom, in an action that is not of desire, there must be the sparkle of doubt. When one actually sees, not theoretically nor verbally, that the action of desire is corrupt, distorted, the very perception is the beginning of that intelligence from which action is totally different. That is, to see the false as the false, the truth in the false, and truth as truth. Such perception is that quality of intelligence which is neither yours nor mine, which then acts. That action has no distortion, no remorse. It doesn't leave a mark, a footprint on the sands of time. That intelligence cannot be unless there is great compassion, love, if you will. There cannot be compassion if the activities of thought are anchored in any one particular ideology or faith, or attached to a symbol or to a person. There must be freedom to be compassionate. And where there is that flame, that very flame is the movement of intelligence.

Be a watcher and be free.

There is a transitional state between deep sleep and waking mode of the mind, called Bija Jagrat in which thought flow and tendencies are yet to take hold on our consciousness. If we can hold on to that state for some time, the undercurrent of it will have its effect al through the day. Every being has this state but because we are unaware it goes unnoticed. Daily we sleep without feeling that we are going into a supernatural state. Similarly we can go into a state of meditation in waking mode of mind. Every human is endowed with that potential but we have to actualize it. For sleeping we don't do any methods. The more naturally we work in waking mode, sleep we will have state happens itself and we will have undisturbed sleep. Similarly meditation happens as naturally as it should be if we have the skill to live a life without conflict. It is the mental conflict that denies us natural happening of meditation in waking mode. So if we want such thing happen to us we have to live a life which is without conflict. But at present all our activity is resulting in mental conflict. So we have to change our way of thinking and life radically if we want to live a life without conflict. Basic needs can be fulfilled but psychological desires cannot be fulfilled. It is the desires that drive us mad with rabid ambition which results in a life with severe mental conflict. Sleep, food, making love with opposite gender(Maithunam),meditation are basic needs of every human being. But we are living in such a culture and way of life is such that during the waking mode of mind with our self centred activity we are doing everything that prevents natural happening of meditation while we are awake. Our culture is preventing us from the natural happening of meditation which is as natural as happening of daily sleep. The structure of society is such that it throws everybody into a stream of sorrow and misery. The society creates guilt if anybody tries to live naturally. Our society, our religions are all anti-life, anti-natural .Once we live a way of life which is against the nature and life we are split and we will have perennial mental conflict. Meditation will not happen to a mind that is split and in a state of conflict .A man with conflict and guilt can easily be enslaved. Our conditioning provides them both. Politicians keep such people enslaved at physical level by denying them bare basic needs of life. The priest at psychological level enslaves the humanity by keeping his mind tied to superstitions, beliefs, dogmas and encourages human to do complicated rituals, entertainment and tourism in the name of religion, inventing methods in the name of meditation, all of which aimed to exploit and enslave the fellow human being. See how we are exploiting fellow human being by denying him basic needs both at physical and psychological levels. No saviour will come and redeem us from all these anomalies. Such belief is just a nonsense. We have to redeem ourselves. We have freedom to watch daily life which is a stream of misery. If you carefully watch you will be an outsider to that stream. That watching of daily life and watching the response of our mind to the interaction outside is self-inquiry. It is such a simple thing to be an outsider to that stream of misery. If you really watch you will never enter into that stream again. If you are a watcher, your mind is not split and is not in conflict and for such a mind meditation happens in waking mode and it becomes as natural as happening of sleep-In meditation is happening spontaneously to any person we are calling him as a saint. He is not a saint, he is just living a natural life and you can also live like that, he is just an example. Be free of all beliefs, dogmas, religions which are nothing but organized beliefs, spontaneous meditation will happen to your mind and you will live a life of joy, love, compassion which is real religiosity.

Concluding remarks by the Author

Self knowledge is a constant process of understanding and so there is nothing like an end to it. It comes about when one begins objectively and goes deeper and deeper into the whole problem of daily living with conflict. Life is action in relationship between you and me and the contents of the mind are revealed only in the mirror of relationship. So don't avoid relationship, don't escape from the world because they are the greatest opportunities to do self-inquiry. Kindly don't think living in isolation and sitting cross legged and trying to do self-inquiry is childish. The learning in self-inquiry is through awareness but not from repetitive activity which memory cultivates which leads to conflict, dullness, insensitivity of mind. We have to observe the contents of the mind without interpreting, verbalizing, censoring, choosing. The observation of a scientist is pure, he never tries to manipulate what is seen. He just note down the facts of his observation. Similar scientific attitude is required in self-inquiry, observing without the interference of ego. Here in the very observation action takes place because once we observe that ambition leads to destruction we never go after it. If we do self-inquiry with passion giving our whole energy to it we comprehend the whole fragmentary activity which is leading us to sorrow and misery. There is no basis for our thought and action if we do not know "who we are". Self-inquiry does not solve our problems on a retail basis, it helps us to know that we are not the mind and in that revelation a great transcendence happens and we touch the mystery and message beyond the mind. Suddenly all problems becomes insignificant and slowly they evaporate. Then an existential order happens to our mind and wherever there is order there is love. So self-inquiry leads a life of love. When there is love in relationship this very earth is heaven. When there is no love in relationship this very earth is hell which is the case now. So do self-inquiry and claim the heaven which is your birth right.